Play-a-Song®

Adventure Songs

W9-BIK-992

Battery Information
Includes 3 replaceable AAA batteries (UM-4 or LR03).

Battery Installation
1. Open battery door with small flat-head or Phillips screwdriver.
2. Install new batteries according to +/- polarity. If batteries are not installed properly, the device will not function.
3. Replace battery door; secure with small screw.

Battery Safety
Batteries must be replaced by adults only. Properly dispose of used batteries. See battery manufacturer for disposal recommendations. Do not mix alkaline, standard (carbon-zinc), or rechargeable (nickel-cadmium) batteries. Do not mix old and new batteries. Only recommended batteries of the same or equivalent type should be used. Remove weakened or dead batteries. Never short-circuit the supply terminals. Non-rechargeable batteries are not to be recharged. Rechargeable batteries are to be removed from device before being charged. Rechargeable batteries are to be charged under adult supervision. If batteries are swallowed, in the USA, promptly see a doctor and have the doctor phone (202) 625-3333 collect. In other countries, have the doctor call your local poison control center. Batteries should be changed when sounds mix, distort, or become otherwise unintelligible as batteries weaken. The electrostatic discharge may interfere with the sound module. If this occurs, please simply restart the sound module by pressing any key.

Warning: Changes or modifications to this unit not expressly approved by the party responsible for compliance could void the user's authority to operate the equipment.

NOTE: This equipment has been tested and found to comply with the limits for a Class B digital device, pursuant to Part 15 of the FCC Rules. These limits are designed to provide reasonable protection against harmful interference in a residential installation. This equipment generates, uses, and can radiate radio frequency energy and, if not installed and used in accordance with the instructions, may cause harmful interference to radio communications. However, there is no guarantee that interference will not occur in a particular installation. If this equipment does cause harmful interference to radio or television reception, which can be determined by turning the equipment off and on, the user is encouraged to try to correct the interference by one or more of the following measures: Reorient or relocate the receiving antenna. Increase the separation between the equipment and receiver. Connect the equipment into an outlet on a circuit different from that to which the receiver is connected. Consult the dealer or an experienced radio TV technician for help.

Conforms to the safety requirements of ASTM F963-03.

Product and sound element design, engineering, and reproduction are proprietary technologies of Publications International, Ltd. Patents pending.

Published by Louis Weber, C.E.O., Publications International, Ltd.
7373 North Cicero Avenue   Ground Floor, 59 Gloucester Place
Lincolnwood, Illinois 60712   London W1U 8JJ

Customer Service: 1-800-595-8484 or customer_service@pilbooks.com

www.pilbooks.com

8 7 6 5 4 3 2 1
ISBN-10: 1-4127-8463-8
ISBN-13: 978-1-4127-8463-4

Illustrated by Victoria Miller, Dave Aikins, and A & J Studios

publications international, ltd.

Good Morning to You

Good morning to you,
Good morning to you,
Good morning, dear friend,
Good morning to you.

When I See Boots A-Climbin'

When I see Boots a-climbin',
 When he's upside down in his tree,
He looks so very funny 'cause
 His eyes are where his chin should be!

Big Blue River

Way down upon the Big Blue River,
  Far, far away.
That's where we'll find fruit for our basket,
  We've made for Abuela's birthday!

Come on, *¡Vámonos!*

Are you ready to explore? C'mon!
  ¡Vamos! ¡Arriba!
Doo Doo Doo Doo Duh Dora, all right!
  Doo Doo Doo Doo Duh Dora, oo! oo!
Doo Doo Doo Doo Duh Dora
  Doo Doo Doo Doo Duh Dora, let's go!
Dora Dora Dora the Explorer, Dora!
  Boots and super cool *Exploradora.*
We need your help! Grab your backpack!
  Let's go! Jump in! *¡Vámonos!*
You can lead the way! HEY! HEY!
  Doo Doo Dora, Doo Doo Duh Dora
  Doo Doo Dora, Doo Doo Duh Dora
Swiper, no swiping! Swiper, no swiping!
  Oh mannn!
Dora the Explorer!

Over the Mountain and Through the Woods

Over the mountain and through the woods,
 To Big Blue River we go.
Map shows the way every day,
 And says to catch stars as we go.

Arms and Shoulders, Legs and Feet

Arms and shoulders, legs and feet, legs and feet,
Arms and shoulders, legs and feet, legs and feet,
Reach and climb and rise up high,
Arms and shoulders, legs and feet, legs and feet.

Twinkle, Twinkle, Little Star

Twinkle, twinkle, little star, how I wonder what you are.
   Up above the world so high, like a diamond in the sky.
Twinkle, twinkle, little star,
   How I wonder what you are.

Mi Amigo Boots

Oh, *mi amigo*, Boots,
    He is a friend to me,
His favorite things are his red boots,
    And climbing in a tree!

It's Raining, It's Pouring

It's raining, it's pouring,
   We need what Backpack's storing.
We have to stay warm and dry,
   So we can keep exploring.

This Is the Way We Stop Swiper

This is the way we stop Swiper,
Stop Swiper, stop Swiper.
This is the way we stop Swiper,
From swiping our umbrella.

Splash, Splash, Splash!

Where, oh where, are the great big puddles?
Where, oh where, are the great big puddles?
Where, oh where, are the great big puddles?
Let's find one and go, splash, splash, splash!

Polly Wolly Doodle

Oh, we caught some stars, and kept Swiper away,
Sing Polly wolly doodle all the day.
Now to pick the fruit, we're on our way,
Sing Polly wolly doodle all the day!